MAY IS AN ISLAND

Books by Jonathan Johnson

Poetry
Mastodon, 80% Complete
In the Land We Imagined Ourselves
May Is an Island

Nonfiction
Hannah and the Mountain

MAY IS AN ISLAND

Jonathan Johnson

Carnegie Mellon University Press
Pittsburgh 2018

ACKNOWLEDGMENTS

Grateful acknowledgment is made to the editors of the magazines in which these poems, or versions of them, first appeared:

American Literary Review: "Alone and with Others"; *Epoch*: "From a Second-Story Café," "Young"; *Gettysburg Review*: "After Autumn," "The Missing Color"; *Georgetown Review*: "Essay on Kindness as Inactivity"; *The Missouri Review*: "Balloon," "I've Turned from the Distant," "Interiority," "Longing Is Not Desire," "To Whoever May Care for Me Dying," "In the Year of Gorillas"; *New Ohio Review*: "Dispensation," "Point of View"; *Passages North*: "For the Finder of My Days"; *Pleiades*: "Living"; *Ploughshares*: "Out Far Enough"; *Poetry Northwest*: "Of Her Offering"; *Prairie Schooner*: "In Green Park in the rows . . ."; *Rattle*: "Night Drive at Twenty-Five and Twenty-Six through Tunnels of Oak"; *Sewanee Review*: "Suddenly Seeing in Absent Sandstone How It Will Be"; *Smartish Pace*: "Don't Mistake Them," "Empirical Fallacy"; *Witness*: "Cascades," "Glenelg, First Night"

Book design by Samantha Mack

10 9 8 7 6 5 4 3 2 1

CONTENTS

Foreword

Afterword

∽

Have you built your ship of death . . . ?

—D. H. Lawrence

FOREWORD

DISPENSATION

We are mistaken to suppose the dead want
us to walk out at night and stare alone
into the dark horizon. Thinking them just beyond
the wind, we stand facing the cold and waves
like a shore pine shaped to absence.
We speak to clouds we know only
by a lack of stars. We count ourselves
with them, keeping our backs to town
or gazing down shore at its small lights
with abstracted affection. But the dead
don't ask for our loneliness.
We confuse loyalty to what is not
with loyalty to them while trying not to shiver.
In fact, our little errand was done when we heard
the crescendo and diminuendo of those waves
visible only in the white of their ending
and thought what little we perceive of beauty's extent.
Beyond that, the dead would send us
to dens of laughter and warm light.
What are you doing out here? they would ask.
There are songs being sung. Take yourself there.
Touch someone's hand. Sit at a table
where someone speaks the name I knew you by.

OUT FAR ENOUGH

For sorrow we have love and the waves dying in.

We can visit our lives in the country of winter trees and blue ruin.

For the nameless we have silence.

Where tenderness runs out there is tenderness.

A trail descends into the next glen.

Our anti-muse's hair is the color of loam.

For gospel she has shelved volumes of everything we leave unwritten.

For forgiveness she has light from a peat fire, rain on small windows.

IN MAY

Behind him the car, fifteen odometer miles
and black as newly minted nothing yesterday
when he pulled from the airport rental lot.
Behind him the villages, croft byres and liveries,
stone walls and stone walls' geometry across
heather and grass, a lease without ink, contrails
thinned in dissemination as powder of bone
on the moving sea. Behind him the moving sea,
every last hour before the slow rise of this
mountainside like mountainsides she'd described
when he was a boy and he had imagined
and neither had seen. Behind him her handwriting
in pencil some years some in pen down margins
beside Wordsworth in typeface inside her
softbound *Prelude.* The one she bought used
from a university bookstore when she was young.
The spine-taped, rubber-banded one she gave him
the first term he taught the seminar. The one
he now fears he's lost—of all the books
why that one with her exclamations of *yes!*
and *Nature as nurse and moral guide* and
the moment in her life she wrote *the sublime*
and everything she said and every phrase
she underlined?—to his compounding grief
somewhere behind him. Behind him the trail,
bunched into switchbacks under blue sunlight
and threading down through spring where sheep
drift as specks from the speck of a sheepdog.

Behind him the distance he crossed to leave the trail,
to come here and lay his back on the slope
for a time with the sky and loll his face
to one side and see the grass this close and hear it
and be happy like he was as her son.

GLENELG, FIRST NIGHT

Gus am bris an là

Out from this croft house opens the comfort
of black mountains and black sea,
black wind flattening black grass,
black granite and black names, names
with sharp shape and names become smooth
black rain, black wind, black sheep
white snowflake specks high on the dead
bracken hill today—*Sheep don't get cold,*
a boy with whom I share seven-hundred years
of people here told me—black tractor, black hay,
black Skye ferry tied to a black pier,
black school, black shop, narrow black road
in cursive down from Ratagan Pass,
black Riverfoot Cottage where the Glenmore
meets the black Sound of Sleat, black sound
of wind at the window, black ceiling
of cloud scrolling fast, black smoke from the chimney,
black heart, black blood in black veins,
black ink in the dark, a hundred and two years
since my great-grandfather slept in this black glen,
my silver car, black out on the black gravel drive,
black lichen on black rock-stacked fence up steep slopes
by hands become dirt, black maple, black grass,
fifteen black white and black collie pups
drowsing at their mothers' black teats,
black peat, black quilt, black pillow, black sheets,
and I, who have never slept here, am back and drift—

no, not drift, touch ground to sleep in the comfort
of black mountains and black sea, the infinity
of color in black, *until the day breaks.*

—for Cousin Catherine

OF HER OFFERING

In the language of lighthouses
two flashes, fourteen seconds,
two flashes means
This is the Isle of May.
The light repeats its phrase
exactly as when someone
in from a black horizon
might have needed it.
Exactly as if the subtext
were still *You are not lost.*
Before it dies
a good language matures
to speak something of love.
Before bed my daughter
parts the curtain and cups her hands
at her temples to shade the glass
from the lamp on the desk
behind her. Five miles out
the light flashes twice.
Without counting she knows
how long to wait
so she'll be answered
when she says, "Good night."

MY MOTHER HAS BECOME A COVE

After all these years, a grotto
of sandstone facing every mood of water.
I refuse to live without her voice
answering mine, if I speak or not,
in the rattle of heart-sized stones
wet in the ebb between waves.
She breathes in the green hemlock,
wind-stunted spruce, pine boughs.
Her face looking on mine lights the horizon
through afternoon graying to evening.
A point. Regard. The distant lighthouse,
the French word for which
I recently learned is the same
for its beam and wonder
if she knew is *phare*.

INTERIORITY

A man allows himself to sink
to his desk before a window
onto the winter sea, to shut his eyes
and feel his sweater sleeve
beneath his cheek, the wood smooth
under his hand, each breath's arrival slow
as the waves he knows are out the window.
He knows snowflakes are lifting
on the updraft just beyond the glass.
He's given up trying to imagine
or remember anything else.
The great story in which he lives now,
the death and tender face and home,
will return for him. He can hear it.

I'VE TURNED FROM THE DISTANT

I've turned from the distant towers of coast to
   where the path turns inland
and follows the track between fence and barley field past
   a six-bottom plow left behind
to take the sun and the wind off the sea and rust
   another season. Twenty years
I have lived apart from the first girl I loved
   and that is how I will go on.
So why am I now remembering how she could be still
   in the close, antique light
through the window on a gray afternoon?
   The violin gave its slow answer
to the lute. Quiet. Soft and Quiet.
   The path entered a wood alongside
a stone byre and deepened to the shaded,
   quick water I'd seen on a map
though somehow hadn't expected, at least not the canopy
   of basswood or beech or the language
of the current breaking little falls over boulders to a ruined mill
   where trees grew to join the wood
through the absent roof. Only stone on stone
   delineated someone's intentions and days.
The sea was somewhere downstream, toward which
   the path returned. To the leaves it could have been
a hundred miles off, they were so calm.
   And when those leaves were behind me
I thought of them, even where the water pooled wide
   at the mouth between banks of alder

and driftwood, sun bleached on the rocks.

   I thought of those leaves until I saw
through low limbs two swans turning slowly
   on that satin water just before the procession
of waves took the river into itself.

LONG

This coast is made of rock and grass.
The sea is made of gray.
The island five miles out is made of rock and grass.
And this day is made of gray.

There is another day
where overcast ends in gold and copper hills
a few degrees high at the horizon and all day
it's been made of gold and copper hills.

I am made of nothing.
I have stepped over fences of stone as someone
walking into the tight, gray weave of nothing.
While over there someone

also made of nothing has walked as sun
along her coast of misty, winter sun.

LONGING IS NOT DESIRE

Longing was never meant to be satisfied.
Alone with the ruins on the grassy promontory,
low sun of early January on the sea,
I long to be alone with the ruins,
low sun of early January on the sea.
When at last I look back, I long to look back,
ruins in silhouette over silhouette of rocks,
some of what's left of the day showing
through former windows. What desire makes
crumbles with the weight of its own creation.
But longing, longing wants most when it has. So forgive me,
when our blankets are spread before the cottage fire
and it's been night after night since I've touched your skin,
if my fingertip lingers along one last seam.

BALLOON

Twine ropes webbing down
to the tiny wicker basket
and tiny sandbags waiting
to be cut loose if the treetops
rise too close, the balloon hangs
to one side above sable brushes,
putty knives and a polished wood
desk easel in the narrow window
of a Latin Quarter art supply.
When I was a boy, my mother
brought home a projector
from the university and showed
The Red Balloon on the wall
of our student family apartment.
I was learning to be tender,
to believe the world's delicate
things reciprocate a boy's affection.
Ballon! Ballon! the boy called,
and the balloon trailed him silently.
I wept when the bullies' stones
burst the taut, bright skin,
and wept on for the empty balloon
even after its compatriots found the boy
and carried him up with their colors
over the rooftops of Paris.
The Red Balloon was gone.
It had shown the boy his life and died.
Halfway across this city of wrought

and chiseled inanimates, gilded,
glassed, oiled and acryliced objects
meant to elicit adult admiration
and here and there outright pathos,
my daughter will be rising late
in a hotel bed beside her mother,
her stuffed lamb threadworn and smelling
of old fevers, juice and soap, smelling
of her own skin on her starched pillow.
She'll be stepping from the shower,
steam rising from her shoulders.
My mother loved me like that,
remembered the waking child's smell
on my skin and hair, my smooth
renewal stepping from bath to towel.
Me, of all people in the world,
and now she's gone.
Down from the shop window
the model balloon is light
as memory and fragile, but it's safe
in crumpled newspaper in a white box
I carry through streets
and over bridges as the sky,
as if in invitation, breaks open.

IN THE YEAR OF GORILLAS

The first I knew of Anya's fear
was holding her before *Blue Gorilla*,
some undergrad's painting
in a gallery on Washington Street.
I've forgotten what she said
but recall her arms tightening
around my neck and shoulder, her legs
gripping my torso. She must
have been three. There were nightmares
and the book she insisted on
sleeping with every night, tiptoeing
gorilla holding a flashlight
on the cover. I know
she was three because later that year
my mother would be done
with everything she'd done for years
not to die and three was the last
my mother saw of Anya, pirouetting
on the great stage of bedroom
revealed when my mother raised
her heavy eyelids. Was it
even a minute, that final recital,
one life's last vision of a body turning?
Wonderful my mother said before letting
her lids sink. Anya must have
been three because the two photos
of her turning—sneaker toe to
raised-hand fandango pivot in one,

in the other a moment later, her arms

out like a galaxy's spirals, dress

twirling, her face already half around

to the direction she's spinning—

were taken in Spain six weeks

after my mother was ash

and could never see Anya again.

And she must have been three

as that was the trip Anya's mother

and I took her to the Madrid Zoo

and told her we didn't have to go

to the gorillas. But she wanted to.

I remember her standing at the glass,

us in the dark, the gorilla out

in leaf shadow and sunlight,

Buddha-big and still, sitting

beside a trickle of water, hands

with creases like old, black vinyl.

FOR THE FINDER OF MY DAYS

You named the Opel Blueberry
and we drove her deep into winding twilight.
The descent was longer than I'd expected.
The sea when it finally showed, black
between the lowest of many steep hills,
was like the bottom of the sea.
I tell you this now because you were three.
We parked on the beach. A few other cars.
Wooden boats hulled over on the sand.
Spanish village in the night behind us.
I thought I'd found, if not my life,
my life's aftermath. A few lights from
where the bay curved away fell apart
in the water. Blanched with miles of sleep,
a drowsy brightness in your mother's arms,
you charmed us the biggest room from the young
woman keeping the empty inn of the moon.
In the morning from the rooftop terrace we saw
the world had risen again, umber, dusty green
and terra-cotta down to the blue Opel
and sand. The sand on which I'd watch you search—
blue hat, red bucket—for shells and sticks
and the smoothest rocks that now, ten years on,
were the strewn doubloons of my lost history.

INVITATION TO MY DAUGHTER
TO A FAVORITE PLACE

Escort yourself when the sky is low and soon
to rain through a cemetery I know. An estate of days.
So many old trees and new trees to choose.
A pond. Like a cemetery from the novel
our living writes. Once, where the road's still dirt,
an old man on a red moped trailed slowly past
me that gas smoke smell of mopeds everywhere.
Walking, I watched him in his cap, going on
as each of us and everything does. And now
the rain begins. Nothing, not the leaves,
not the stones or grass, not the narrow pavement,
not the back of the slow-turning duck, is wet yet.
Feel these first drops on your face, so soft
you're not sure, whenever you might come.

THE MISSING COLOR

The spectrum healed seamlessly.
That autumn arrived without a scar.
Sun shone trumpets through aspen
and because it rained at night
the grass grew soft again.

No one spoke the missing color's name.
Why would they? Mallards turned
in the still pool. You could swirl paint
and get anything, lift it
and touch your brush to banners
cracking above the castle.

Mums blossomed over the broken garden.
Who could call their efforts incomplete?
Light through a breaking wave,
velvet off a lacquered piano, the warm
trapezoid on the afternoon floor
lacked—but what?

There's nowhere to point.
And when the remembering mind
is gone, it will be
as if the missing color
never was. But it was.
It was everywhere.

AFTER AUTUMN

                    Snow
falls as leaflets from a great,
gray zeppelin, but the field
has already surrendered.
The trees teach us it's all right
to be done. And how
to be seen through
and remain lovely.

Grief is not resistance.
Its dreams turn the lake
white and empty the house
of even hushed voices. The sun
goes; the sun comes.
There is no waiting. The end
of hope is the end of fear.
When snow falls again

it takes the distance into itself.
It takes color. Leaving the shape
of grace. Which is the sorrow
of the world close around us.

EMPIRICAL FALLACY

So the trees don't branch
to such improbable heights
for us and the creatures
bringing their small, unafraid
silhouettes out into the dusk
to bend to the grass and eat
this close know nothing of forgiveness.
Grace needs no intention.
So the daisies don't mean
anything by blossoming but make
their white fabric whether or not
the lovers from another year return.
So our contentment beside a pond
is not the pond's design,
is no gift of still reflection
or distant crow's caw or frog's
occasional glunk, is nothing
left by the thinning, morning fog.
Perhaps once in a life a feather
falls slowly and exactly into
easy, midair reach.
More often, leaves. Neither,
we're told, are offerings.
Nor is rain. Nor
are large, descending stars
of snow that enter our loneliness.
So the world cannot love us.
That just makes its breeze, cool

from time spent traveling so far
over water to arrive on the face
staring out over land's crumpled end,
all the more worthy of our trust.

ONCE I'D WATERED EVERY FLOWER IN THE GARDEN . . .

Once I'd watered every flower in the garden
and stood to wonder how many more years

they'd keep coming up with their god gone
and would it be so bad if it turns out

we'd been made, we'd all been made,
and left as our perished maker's memorial,

I wanted overwhelmingly to be elsewhere,
as though if I stayed I would know

a loneliness we never outlive, all the loss
in the sun-paled pink of roses, orange

of leaning poppies, shedding blossoms of peonies,
and with the voice of their lost god who loved me

and wanted me out in the world if the world
is where I preferred to be, every flower

spoke with sympathetic urgency, Go!
Yes, I answered. Though where I couldn't say.

LIVING

Enjoy this sandwich. While the sun
lasts. Wet goat cheese on lettuce.
Every bite. Cranberries. Pear. Snap
of pine nuts. I mean *this*
sandwich. Under *this* sun. Someone
stopped on his way once. Say,
a thousand years ago. A desert.
He sat down and ate something.
Lamb. Maybe even a pear. Damp
white cheese from goats in the village.

SAMOS ISLAND ENDING IN EASTER

Friday after sundown, men carry the icon from church to square on a flower-
canopied, candle-spiked bier.

Bulbs of electric flame hold in sea wind that pulls across blossoms to lift a few petals
away.

"Stay." The woman takes my hand in the crowd. "They will come from all five
churches."

Palms rise to their tossing fronds and the stone lion presides over old beards
and the gold robes of priests converging

before the holy, unflinching faces borne aloft, out into Passion one night a year.

Turns out, faith does fine without belief. The tears bloom cold and clean through my
own bare austerity.

The waves arrive in centuries belonging to no one's Kýrie eléison. *Kýrie eléison,*
for somewhere else is forever's bankrupt asylum across the darkness and
traveling lights.

Closer sheets move and stay against skin and someone allows someone in for the
fifty-billionth first time.

Grace here comes jagged and bright, tiny as the key to a stone cottage in the hills
among the concrete of half-finished villas.

Through Great Sabbath into another night, a gale off the Aegean rattles the
shutters and smells of olive wood burning in stoves.

If debt's a sovereign, let this be his far, unseen province. Old women's hands break
bread untouched by the knife and children bring it to table in baskets.

Kýrie washes its song over *refrain*, *eléison* over *abstain*. The wisdom of joy is in its
insistence.

Down in the mostly empty tavern, three old men strum and sing and smoke into the last midnight.

In the morning, sun. A few small fishing boats tied off along the quay. Most up on stilts, awaiting summer and paint.

WANTING OTHERS TO SEE BEAUTY IN THINGS AND TO ASSOCIATE THOSE THINGS WITH ME

Little comet the streetlamp calls
coming into my orbit burn
awhile in my light

A GOSPEL

The world speaks everything to us.

—William Stafford

A man kneels to paint the hydrant
at Third and Michigan. At his little altar
of care he carefully strokes the brush
on the red, careful not to touch the gold
of the four bolt plugs—nose, ears, topknot.

This must be a scheduled task. Routine.
Layers of paint over iron like thin growth rings.
The hydrant looked fine before,
but here he is, brightening it.
He wears blue latex gloves and a bill cap.

He dips the brush in a smooth, silver can.
He has a piece of foam for a kneeling board.
He bends a little to see his work.
And then he's gone. The hydrant
stands at the day's bright center.

A MARRIAGE

The kite was a too-sophisticated confusion
of spacer bars and twine, a beautiful
fabric, black and orange and yellow,
a rippling chevron rising fast toward gray,
cool summer clouds above the beach.
Then it spun, and his attempts at correction
overcorrected and it swirled and banged
nose down hard on the sand.
And again. Bang. And again,
ripple, swirl, spin. Bang.
She'd hold it as he walked away, to the end
of the lines, release it when he nodded.
The wind and surf were too loud for their voices.
Up! Lean, lean away, swirl, ripple down,
bang. Bang. Bang. Then once, splash.
She stood just above the waves' reach
in her good leather sandals
and waited as it slogged in.
All of this was adversely affecting his mood.
They should have bought something simple.
Something that would actually fly the first
or second or what was this anyway,
the fifth time out for Christ's sake?
he complained as he wound the string, collapsed
the two wings around the center bar
and shoved the kite back in its sheath.

You want to be good at things right away,
she said, not unkindly. She compared him
to their daughter. Added that at least
it was cool down here, in the breeze,
after such a hot day. They walked
back up the dunes, through a narrow margin
of woods to the car. There, when
he had the key in the ignition
and was about to pull from the sandy shoulder
into the road, she unbuttoned her shorts.
Slid them without preamble or remark
down to her bright ankles.
What are you doing? he asked.
Thought I should change into jeans,
she said and didn't hurry collecting them
from the back seat or sitting back down.
The time she took to pull them on and buckle,
her smile was barely there, but it was.
And thereby did she rescue his dampened spirits
and launch them again, for the rest of the day.

POINT OF VIEW

The father doesn't say so, but he's miffed.
He does say, "That guy shouldn't be there,"
and holds his stare on the head
bobbing along in the cobalt beyond
the sandbar's yellow. He doesn't say,
Not with this much wind and chop
and those currents, and those signs by the parking lot!
He doesn't say, Now I'll have to watch him and worry.
"He shouldn't be out that far?"
the daughter asks, eager to concur.
The mother says, "Maybe it's the Floater.
But I've never seen her here before."
The drowning man is the only one who knows
he is drowning. He cannot lift his arms,
cannot make his lungs form any sound but gasps.
The beach is too far; his feet can't find
the sandbar. The family doesn't know
they are seeing him die, even when he's flat
he seems to be floating. The father's such a worrier.
That's all this is. And he's making his daughter
anxious again—and even his wife—staring out
with his hand shading his eyes.
The guy's just relaxing, like the Floater.
I'll count and see if he doesn't
lift his head to take a breath.
"He's just floating?" the daughter asks.
"Maybe he's on his back," the mother says.
The drowning man is deep in his mind,

now, still himself, still in possession
of his memories, of the faces of his long-gone
parents, of his phone numbers, of the word "toast,"
though he no longer knows or fears. The father holds
the daughter's boogie board but people have drowned here
attempting rescue and surely that guy'll be any second
taking a breath. He's so hard to see,
rocking in those little swells. *God! This is*
irresponsible, floating like that. But he's not
raising his head to breathe. His head was
just bobbing along. He's fine. "Is he
on his back?" the mother asks. The girl does not know
not to expect this to be as all right
as things in reality are always all right.
Even when the man slips from sight
and the sirens close in, she doesn't know
what she has seen. What she has seen
will only be a man's dying in the memory
soon to begin, and even then, for days
she'll say, "I don't understand."

ESSAY ON KINDNESS AS INACTIVITY

Arguably one of the greatest kindnesses I ever did
was not killing someone. I wanted to.
Not really. But really. It would have been easy,
a cinch. He's a drinker and deep-sea fisherman.
Pretend we're still friends, a little push
into the cold northern waters he trawls,
an hour before the frantic radio call.
A cinch. People do that sort of thing.
Not doing it I have always considered baseline,
but that doesn't mean it's no accomplishment.
One I'd argue does fit the definition of kind,
at least *a* definition. Because of that ongoing decision
this guy still goes fishing, knows the taste of grilled chicken,
can think about what it's like making love to a woman.
What he did to my life's not really the point—
though it's ongoing. Who doesn't think he's done right,
mostly? New research is showing those denied revenge
frequently believe they'd be happier if they could take it.
And that they're wrong. Think of Achilles
dragging dead Hector behind his chariot for days
through dust and beach sand. Like a job.
Rise, clock in, drag Hector, get up, do it again.
There is no satisfaction that we imagine.
I've seen someone drown, the quiet of it
because the lungs tighten before they go under.
Who needs that? Plus, as I say, he's alive.
And this kindness is also to my wife, whom I love,
who is married to a man who has never killed anyone.

And my daughter, whose dad's no killer. Come on.
This kindness of not having killed a man
is also, so obviously, a kindness to me—
free mind, free body, drifting in my little dory,
oars tucked in, rocking, slosh of wavelets,
keeping an eye I don't get too far from shore.

THE SPIDER IN MY WINDOW

I would not kill my only companion
in this stone cottage against wind and rain
and gray off the sea and up the glen,
though there's no counting those in town
I've crushed or smeared or drowned.
So we're both better here, far away and alone.

MEAT

There's nowhere to avert your gaze
in Athens' Varvakios Agora from
white ladders of ribs curled around emptiness,
muscled legs sliced into splayed pages, apron smear,
rows of slick maroon organs, flop
and thwack across chopping block, the sheen
and teeth and bulging eyes of skinned heads
dangling side by side by side by side
from the hook-hung carcasses of all
that's left of everything each creature needed
to be its own self, the rest beside in stacks
and strung in ropes of knotted sausage.
Too late I saw my mistake, leading two
fourteen-year-old girls, my daughter and daughter's
best friend, through the high-covered narrow
confusion of faces, inked price cards, scrutiny,
and scents of iron and bleach. Not that it was them
through the long, pressed passage back to daylight
I'd failed to protect. The problem is not
that the metaphor's old and worn, but that it's
no metaphor at all. Like recently in the café
I frequent enough to have become friendly
with a fellow regular a few years premature
in being elderly. A stroke, he told me,
hunched over his wheeled walker through the door
I held open. His hooded sweatshirt hangs loose
with the name of a prestigious university
he told me his daughter once attended.

Sometimes when I meet with a student at my table
he positions himself to listen in. Eagerly
he returns my little pleasantries so that
I've come to feel generous giving his soft, plump hand
more of a little hold than a shake. His gray whiskers
grow thick for days. And that's how and as far
as it usually goes, isn't it, with such acquaintances.
Such ordinary calls to generosity. Except
last Thursday. Music night at the café.
A table of my friends and friends' kids fresh
from karate at their dojo down the street.
One flushed ten-year-old out of her gi
and into sweatpants and a snug tank top.
And I saw the way he positioned himself, perched,
on the stool nearby. I knew
even before he leaned in to ask her her age.
The knowing remained a bright blade outside myself.
(I had been kind. He had been lonely.) I did nothing.
The girl was oblivious in her flesh.
The thought of everyone's skin doubled back
on itself and peeling was mine.

THE ADJUNCT

Look, this is where I grew up,
these beaches you've written yourself onto
for two bucks a word, that big old Foursquare
you're having renovated with the period-correct,
subway-tile bathroom, the park where your kid
goes down the twisty slide—*mine.* And they were
mine long before they were yours.
You come here, the hiring committee's darling
de jour, set up shop at your café table
three mornings a week, right where anyone
coming or going gets to see you
at your little stack of oh-what's-he-reading? books
and your student conferences, just two chums over coffee,
and your tenure and your off-to-France
next year for sabbatical and your new Subaru,
not the one you had in graduate school going on
three-hundred thousand miles (ha, ha!)
you worried every time you cranked the engine
and with the noise you listened to for signs
it was getting worse. My noise is getting worse,
not that it's any concern of yours. You've got
that hiring committee for the next new darling.
And she's out there, you'll find her,
what a search! Like the six of you are surf-
launching one of those big wooden rescue boats
with sets of long oars, pushing out through
breaking waves and fog. Searching, searching
for the hero out in her ship—please,

come in to our little island, tell us
so much we don't know on our
remote little outpost. Look, I'm not saying
any of this is your fault. You're smart,
you had the advantages you had and
not those you didn't. You struggled. You felt
afraid and struggled some more. You took
a look at this place and thought, maybe here.
If they want me, I could want this place.
Lucky you. And I was free to go
and stay gone. To search myself and
keep searching for the little lifeboat to bring
me in on some shore, hero with my satchel
and news of the world. But what you need
to understand is, this is what I have.
I know the names of every street, in order,
between that Foursquare of yours, through the leafy
neighborhood and then through the not leafy
neighborhood with cars on the remains of lawns
all the way up to the campus. I could tell you each
house you pass on your walk. Each one I'll never
afford but where I and not you kissed someone
for the first time and sat beside the death breaths
of someone I'd never known the world without.
Your office is the one with the window, so think of me
as out in that roof- and treetop-scape
you look contemplatively over when you take
a moment's satisfied pause between your two upper-

division courses and grad thesis advisees.
Think of me like your kids, if that helps,
who were born here. Who, if they want
to be like you, will have to leave you.

UNEXPECTEDLY

The girl's dog dies.
In the back of the car
speeding through the night.
The girl in bed, waiting for news.
The parents must drive back
from the vet in the dark.
Twenty-five miles of forest
broken by the thin beginning
of what will be light, out
on the horizon of water.
The girl is waiting inside
on the landing to ask if
the dog is okay. The girl's
usual disposition is even and sweet.
Like her dog's. A single bark
at the sliding glass door
to come in. The fierce *Don't*
and rage in the girl's clenched fists
and eyes staring him down
were not the anguish her father,
moving to embrace her, expected.
At the vet's the dog's body
had been heavy as a human's
in the blanket sling. Her back
was so big, all three—mother,
father, and girl—could scratch
deep in her fur and sing
about an itchy back, a song

the mother had invented
just for her. *What's wrong?*
four and a half years ago
the father had asked into
the back seat of the same car,
driving the dog home
over snowy mountains.
The dog's head was a puppy's
in the girl's lap, and the girl
was weeping. *She's perfect.*
Now, the mother says *Let her go*
when the girl rushes past them
and out the door. Upstairs,
there is a moment in which
the father thinks he hears coyotes
screaming high-pitched through
night ending in the forest
before he knows it's the girl,
the sound of being loved
by the dog leaving her body.

THESE ARE THE TERMS

There's no end to the mourning.
This nestling world waits, tendon thin
neck upstretched, blue skin enormous
eyes shut blind, and its vast tiny mouth
locked open. Trembling bowl held skyward.
Even now. Every word of adoration and song
from your own mouth spills down
to disappear with all the moments and love
you've fed away already, living your life.
And yet. Walk old neighborhoods.
Sooner or later there's a new, slender tree,
planted in your absence, already leafing
above your head. It will be many years
before any mother makes her nest there.
By then someone will have planted another.
Seen-through sapling. Fragile in the breeze.
There is no end to the joy.

YOUNG

Keats sells me an iPhone at the Verizon store.
I think I have a couple 5s left in the back, he says. *They're free*
if you sign up. He checks and sure enough.
I'd come only to trade my dying old clamshell for another,
but it's just ten bucks more a month if I get a data plan.
I ask if it's good, working here. *Ideal,* he smiles his shy chagrin.
There's not much traffic. Sometimes I have all day for lines.

And Fanny. Ah, Fanny, Fanny, Fanny . . .
She has this tree, rooting into her hip
and branching leafless up the side of the small of her back.
I've never been one for tattoos, but when
he lifts her dancing and she is suspended there
and she looks down at him and he looks up
into her face—her delicate, adoring face—
and the hem of her camisole rises from the waist of her skirt
to reveal that tree, it's easy to believe
it will never pass into nothingness.

SUDDENLY SEEING IN ABSENT SANDSTONE
HOW IT WILL BE

Mostly time is slow about amputating
our lives from us. Our fifteen-year-old sits
at the table where she was four, debating
how many weeks in our hometown will fit
into her summer and we let her win.
My young body and your young body are gone.
Years, we don't see some people we call friends.
Our college has buildings where there was lawn.

Today though, back here without you, I walked
the island shore path out to the spire
on which we sat with our pizza slices. Our Rock.
Jetty in the waves. Perch over flat water.
Where the iced brush parted, out past the snow,
I saw what some storm had done.

OH BLESSED MORTALITY

There were ducks. Geese.
  Still, black waters of August.
Over the stone footbridge
  to the tiny island
in the cemetery pond,
  on the grass under
three pines joined at the trunks,
  a few birch and a maple,
the couple lay on their backs.
  Clouds came and went.
When I walked past
  all I could see of them
was the tops of their heads,
  side by side, their leisurely legs,
their bare, young feet.

DON'T MISTAKE THEM

Birch rise, skeletons, still, of leafy sky
and just enough sunlight reaches the grass
on which he once composed. Absence disguised
as a house keeps its claim on her address.
The pond remains the pond, though unwalked to.
They're gone. They had their time. In the restaurant
down the street, don't mistake them for these two,
talking of those they married (a little) and kids (a lot)
and lingering politely on, abridging
years since the year they made what they called love,
about which they needn't speak, the unhinging
each knows the other so capable of.
And don't mistake them for us, each alone,
later, imagining the other walking home.

FROM A SECOND-STORY CAFÉ

Look at them down there in sunset gold off the gray stone walls and glass
shimmering off cobblestones.

The women. In black tights, skirts and scarfs. Boots, jackets.

Sometimes their tights are white. Some hold hands with their fellas. Their guys.

Some hold an elbow. Some walk in rows. Some alone.

A red pony tail. A purse. A long, black wool coat. Jeans. Shoulder packs. Spilling
black hair.

Weight shifting from boot to boot, little kick of her heel on the opposite

toe as she talks to a guy holding a *Free Tours in English* umbrella.

A tuck of that hair behind her ear. A point of her hand down the street. A
laugh.

Winter hats on all those scents of hair. Earmuffs. Earmuffs!

Little buds in ears, filling them with private songs of public privacy.

Walking. Walking. A cold cheek. A nose. Gloved fingers wrapped around a
cardboard coffee cup.

Ah, lovability, spilling through the world's streets as shop lights come on.

Lovely lovability below, I offer no defense for myself at my perch.

I've been ten days without you, wife, who teaches yourself to me in every one of
them,

layers of fabric over all that soft skin.

IN GREEN PARK IN THE ROWS . . .

In Green Park in the rows
of—are they mossy sycamore?
hard to tell in the hazy chill light
of a leafless London morning—
I've found you again,
though you're asleep by now, I suppose.
It's easy, this love. Every time,
I need only wait, and there we are—
an empty bench.

NIGHT DRIVE AT TWENTY-FIVE AND TWENTY-SIX THROUGH TUNNELS OF OAK

Each house
we chose
was us
our clothes

back on
our desire dwindled
to lawn
and dappled shingles

our lives
and love made
antique glass.

Now I drive
that neighborhood
in search of us.

CASCADES

One day every memory
of whatever night
this is will be gone.
I row out from my fire
and my fire fades
back into spruce.
Silhouettes of high boughs
sink into the ridgeline's
rising silhouette.
Jupiter's reflection keeps
smooth pace in water
beside me. Moonrise descends
into this narrow valley.
Cascades fall from my oars
with every lift, the perishing
infinity of a white silver I
never knew water contained.

THE MACLURES OF GLENELG

Somewhere a ways up the glen
    some two dozen of them assemble, sit
        on the wool-dandered grass, stand,
            or lean against a dry-stacked stone wall

and look at me a hundred years
    the other side of the camera's black, iris glass.
        They've been shearing. The burly man
            with the fleece half peeled from the sheep

draped over one of his splayed legs
    grips the shears and holds a pipe in his teeth,
        in his mouth, in his beard. The smell
            of tobacco. Sheep shite. Sharp heather.

I know they're a ways up the glen
    because I've been there, where ridgeline
        rises from the long parabola of moorland
            to occupy much of the sky,

as it does behind them. Each of the three women
    amid their men's hat brims, tweed vests,
        coats and caps attaches herself to someone.
            Hands around a ruffle-collared child.

Shoulder against that man's elbow sleeve. Hip
    behind the shoulder of the burly one
        with the half-sheared sheep in his lap.
           She's far too young for her cane,

but whatever the misfortune—mismatched legs,
    a fall, maybe polio—it's lost now, at least to me.
        What endures, though, through her closed lips,
           is the only smile I see for certain

among all those ample beards.
    When I stood in the barnyard with my
        manila folder of notes and an old family tree,
           on my lips the two names

I'd just found in the village cemetery,
    and came that moment to realize the freckled woman
        with whom I was speaking was my cousin,
           she smiled like that. Catherine.

I apologized for interrupting her
    and the two men with whom she'd
        been shearing. *They'll take any excuse
           for a break*, she teased them,

looked back at me, shook her head,

    smiled that hidden smile again and said, *Cousins,*

        while we stood in the sun in our amazement.

            Later, at the kitchen table her father, Uisdean,

placed his weathered finger on the man

    at the photo's front and center. *Your great-grandfather,*

        he said. *My uncle Don.* Catherine's mum, Christine,

            said something in Gaelic they all would have known,

and he slid the photo across the table for me

    to keep. *We lost track of that branch*

        some time ago. I explained my grandparents

            died young in '62. *Ah,* he said.

Just, *Ah.* As in, That explains that then,

    the only account required of me for what had been

        nearly fifty years' silence. I was forty-one,

            hearing my origin story as the self-invention

of the young, beardless man behind

    and around whom the others seem to assemble

        some time before 1911. Just a mustache.

            Hat brim up-curled on one side like a cowboy.

No tweed vest or coat over his collarless shirt.
    He's been working. He folds his arms,
        tucks one foot under the knee of his other leg
            outstretched on the grass and looks

right here, long after the crossing soon
    to Canada, the Vancouver taxi company,
        long after the move down to California, long after
            the company sold to a Pakistani family

who kept the name for business reasons—
    those Scots and their reliability.
        Once, I glimpsed a MacLure's Cabs Prius
            turning inland from a Vancouver quay.

Now, when Catherine's husband Donnie ignites
    the dead heather on the rolling steppe
        of his croft high above the house, I expect
            slow flame through tiny leaves and blossoms,

but they blaze up into insistent wind.
    Flame pushes. Skips. Through yellowed grass
        and bracken to more browned heather.
            Beside him, I paddle down the forward flame.

Eye-sting of smoke through long, merciless gusts.
We beat the flares while fire-flood snakes
and the black ground smolders behind.
I imagine fire opening across the dry muir

to forest, burning down to the sea and up
until snowy crags around us. I remind myself,
Donnie's a crofter *and* in the fire brigade.
He must know what he's doing.

But when at last we lean sooty and spent
on our paddle poles and watch the back edge burn
in obedient, little flames, he of few words says,
A while there I thought it would get away.

I try to match his nonchalance. *That would a been bad.*
Awk, no, he shrugs. *You're away,*
I'd a blamed you. Tell me, for all this,
do you suppose it's too late to trade

Johnson for MacLure, or at least write
under the name, my mother's, who also died young
but unknowingly left me this, her unknown place?
Sitting outside a suburban American Starbucks,

I tell my wife I think the burly crofter mid-shear

    might be Don's father John, whose heart attack

        building the road to Sandaig Bay, left Ann,

            his much younger wife, a widow.

And perhaps that's her behind him, too young

    for that cane for which the story's been lost.

        Maybe it's for herding the sheep, my wife says.

            I have only a moment to feel an idiot

before more of that day comes rushing forward

    to contain me and the woman pauses from herding

        for a strong, modest smile as if at everything

            I do not know of her life and, now, the little I do.

When I walk the path a ways up the glen,

    my walk makes a companion of everything,

        cold voice of the stream's tiny falls, smooth stone

            of white quartz in my hand, stags emerging tall

from a wood to steep, open heather. The speck

    of a cottage in the distance draws closer. Blue sky.

        Bright snow high on summits. Alone in the sensual

            curve of this land, I am beyond loneliness.

Imagine a woman who might have lived here
     in my stead had our great-grandfather never left.
          In the turn of her torso, the long parabola of moorland
               slopes down to riverbank pasture along the Glenmore.

In her backward glance, wind leans the grass.
     Her eyes' regard, neither sea nor crag
          nor sky can give. Miles above the last croft,
               by a lochan wind leaves the grass to cross,

I come to the abandoned cottage
     where I would take her like a bride.
          The wood and peat are stacked
               beside the hearth there even now.

I would take her for the sun through
     small windows. I would take her—
          except for the story Uisdean tells
               when I return from discovering that cottage.

He tells me it's called *Suardalan*.
     There's an each-uisge in the lochan, he says.
          A water horse. His blue eyes find mine
               then return to dinner. The kids listen.

I listen. The glen comes right to the window
    when he speaks again. A shepherd at Suardalan
        once called, Come up for me, to the water horse,
            and the water horse came, smooth and white,

to leave the blue lochan behind like silk on the heath.
    I would make a pasture, the shepherd said,
        but many of the stones are too heavy.
            As a pony pulls an apple from a hand,

the water horse pulled with her lips
    a heavy stone from the ground. Silently,
        shepherd and water horse worked together.
            She stacked the big stones and he the small

until, within a stone fence of their making,
    the pasture was cleared. Then the water horse
        strode toward her lochan. Wait, the shepherd called.
            She turned her slender neck to look back on him.

Stay, he said. This ground is free of stones.
    I shall fashion a harness and plow and we shall turn
        the dark loam and plant. She looked at him.
            Was it sorrow in her large, brown eyes?

I am lonely, he confessed. Please.
    There is more to do. As a pony takes
        a long stalk of grass from open ground,
            the water horse took the shepherd.

She took him from the pasture beside the cottage
    and returned into the silk of her lochan.
        Uisdean says his father was a shepherd there,
            once, but not the shepherd in this story—

which he told straight; forgive the poetry
    it's become since that family dinner of salmon
        when I'd returned from my walk to the cottage
            and the lochan, full of my desire to take her

who might have lived there in my place.
    Anti-muse. In the turn of whose torso
        the long parabola of moorland slopes down the glen.
        In whose backward glance wind leans the grass.

Whose eyes' regard neither sea nor crag
    nor sky can give. And of whom I have never spoken.
        The weather on my phone shows 10 Celsius and sun
            there at the moment. Four miles above Catherine's,

Suardalan waits, empty, stone walls warming,
    beyond sight most days of anyone. The rule
        for writing there is take the words given willingly
            from the ground by the ghost of the unlived life.

Claim nothing. And stay out of the lochan.
    Breathe your desire not to be lonely. Breathe
        empty the cottage. Centuries, the stream beside
            has spoken the same, unbroken syllable,

loudest in spring, to empty itself down
    into the Glenmore. As down the glen,
        past where Catherine and Donnie will build
            the house in which to raise Megan and Caitlin,

Campbell and Callum, past the field not yet
    a cemetery into which Ann will go at 97,
        a lifetime after losing John (one of the last
            to fill the old kirkyard), the Glenmore empties

itself into the Sound of Sleat beside Riverfoot,
    also empty in the other photo they gave me
        from about the same time, maybe even the same day,
            everyone's off shearing. The old MacLure cottage

between riverbank and sea. Whitewash.
        Thatch roof and stone outbuildings. Peat smoke rises
                after Christine clears our tea plates
                        and sets a brick on the coals for the smell

she says she thought I'd enjoy. This new house is
        still Riverfoot, where she and Uisdean live now
                with Catherine's brother, Ewen. Anabell's away
                        for the salmon farms but will visit on Friday.

Out the back door Uisdean and I walk Moss,
        the old collie, through shore grass and damp,
                gray wind across the rattle of pebble beach
                        while waves tumble in and clouds break open

over the mountains across the narrow sound
        to Skye. Late sunlight gets through in pieces
                on the sea, a man and collie their whole lives
                        here, me and the longing that brought me

beside them, stilled a while. I hereby name
        the life I knew before this glen and continue
                mostly to occupy, Johnson. Her own parents
                        gone, my mother took the name, and began

with it and my father to make the days
    I go on making. Where I am specific. This son.
        This husband, father, friend. Beloved and afraid
            for my exquisite, fragile shelter. But look again

at old Riverfoot, thatch held against gales
    by ropes and poles you can just see in the photo,
        the path down through bracken and velvet grass
            to the river where quick shimmer slows to black

between banks of exposed bedrock and pebble,
    a few boulders and firm sand, wet and rippled,
        just before the sea. No one's in sight, just now,
          to fetch fresh water for the washbasin.

In June, in California, the year after Don's son
    and son's wife die young alcoholics and orphan
        my mother, her brother and sister,
           it looks like rain. 1963. He's eighty.

He writes Flora and Joan, *My Dear Sisters,*
    Just picked up your very welcome letter
        with all the news about Glenelg & the old timers.
        Brought back fresh memories of the good

old times spent there. (I read this at Riverfoot.

Uisdean found it for me in a drawer.)

I often take a mental stroll about the old place

with fond memories, especially before I doze

off to sleep. I think of you all in prayer.

When I was last in Glenelg, Uisdean corrected me;

the only MacLure in the photo for certain is Don.

So they are unfindable. So are we all in the end.

No face. No name. Nights and days

alone up at that shepherd's cottage. Mountains.

Table and chair out in the grass and sun.

Think of the still lochan, Suardalan empty beside.

Fires that burn on the heathered hillsides.

Wind never in the loam hair of a woman

never there. Think of Riverfoot empty

of all the MacLures a ways up the glen.

It's good to rest a while with everyone.

Take a break from one of his last shearings

before he goes, and sit for a photograph,

while behind him, high on the slopes

to which I now return and walk alone,
    when I lift myself from my specific life,
        two sheep graze, tiny and white, and granite
        emerges from the same, steep ground.

ALONE AND WITH THE OTHERS

When I was a boy and no love had yet been lost,
I'd fall almost asleep on a sofa
my grandmother called a davenport. It wasn't
so much the words I held in the afternoon darkness
I made from shutting my eyes and turning my face
to the afghan as the voices. My people. Like a light
here and there on a valley floor at night in the mountains.
Or the mountains themselves, abstracted to their forms
against moonlit sky. That was in Idaho, getting to be
a long time ago now. A small farmhouse,
standing, still, as it sinks into its cellar,
but never again to be lived in. I drifted
with them. The forest began outside at the edge
of a small, close field and went, I thought, forever.
Like those voices in the room around me would,
for all I knew. I know better now, of course,
here, on the far side of a day gone past dusk
in the Scottish Highlands, with family I had yet to find.
My cousin Campbell's about the age I was then.
He and I take turns running the bail wrapper
while his dad backs and swings the tractor's headlights
to load each fresh one. Pull this lever and
the bail spins, round into the black wrap
like a dying star. Cut it with the razor knife
and tuck the end in tight. Pull that lever
to dump, leaving the smell of hay and emptiness
on the turntable, ready for the next. The boy and I
take turns, three bails each. His go is long enough

for me to leave the diesel growl and gear whir

and walk the narrow road alongside the stone wall

with the moon rising over ridgeline and turn

at the gate and cross the fresh cut field that's the floor

of this deep glen to where the moon sinks away

and the voices of the machines are small and far.

How can one life be one life? Where is then?

When I turn and walk back, I make the moon rise again.

AFTERWORD

TO WHOEVER MAY CARE FOR ME DYING

Do what you must.
Swab the raw places
as delicately as you can,
but go on and swab them.
If I wince, I would be clean.
Such work befits those
who can see so little left
between skull and skin
and not think them.
You needn't imagine
if I say I lived once
on the sea, in the wind
and sun. You're not yet born,
I hope, so what's this world?
If there's nothing for the pain
there's nothing. Thank you
anyway for the morphine
dripped from the eyedropper
onto my tongue like communion,
for the pink, wet sponge
small on its plastic stick
and dabbed on my lips,
if that's where we're at.
Thank you for the clean cotton,
for the comb and buttons
for as long as that was possible.
Step outside when you can
to look at light on things.

From this far I don't know
what else may be required;
but if there's a rose
somewhere in the room
won't you bring it to me?
Press its deep, open folds
right up to my nose.
And whatever song you might sing,
please, sing to me.